PEGASUS ENCYCLOPEDIA LIBRARY

Geography

MOUNTAINS

Edited by: Pallabi B. Tomar, Hitesh Iplani
Managing editor: Tapasi De
Designed by: Vijesh Chahal, Anil Kumar, Rohit Kumar
Illustrated by: Suman S. Roy, Tanoy Choudhury
Colouring done by: Vinay Kumar, Kiran Kumari & Pradeep Kumar

CONTENTS

What are mountains?

A mountain is a large elevated area of land with steep, sloping sides and sharp or slightly rounded peaks that extend high above its surroundings. They are made from rocks and Earth. Some mountains have trees growing on their sides and very high mountains have snow on their peaks. Usually, mountains are higher than 600 m. Those less than 600 m are called hills. Mountains are also steeper than hills.

Mountains have the following common features:

- Summit, also called peak or the head of a mountain
- A very steep valley between young mountains, known as a gorge
- A slope

Mountains exist on every continent and even beneath our great oceans. In fact, mountains occur more often in oceans than on land; some islands are the peaks of mountains emerging out of the water!

24 per cent of our planet Earth is covered with mountains. Mountains cover 64 per cent of Asia, 25 per cent of Europe, 22 per cent of South America, 17 per cent of Australia, and 3 per cent of Africa. Mountains make up one-fifth of Earth's landscape.

The term mountain refers to a single peak. A series of mountains is called a **mountain range**. They are long chains or groups of mountains. They are usually 1,000 or more miles long.

The Rocky Mountains and the Himalayan Mountains are examples of mountain ranges.

A group of mountain ranges is called a mountain system. For example, the **mountain systems** of the United States include the Rockies and the Appalachians.

Types of mountains

Basically, there are five types of mountains:

1. Fold Mountains (Folded mountains or Complex mountains)
2. Fault-block Mountains (Block mountains)
3. Dome Mountains
4. Volcanic Mountains
5. Plateau Mountains

The Rocky Mountain Range

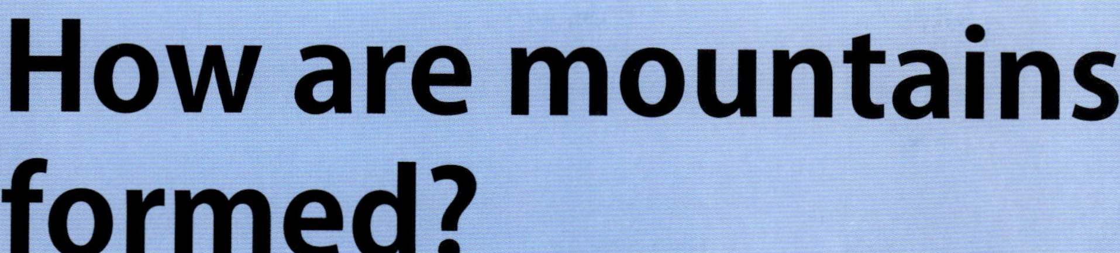

How are mountains formed?

Mountains are formed over long periods of time by strong forces working inside the Earth. Most scientists uphold that most of the mountains are formed by forces of heat and pressure present inside the Earth. These forces cause movements inside the Earth and changes in the Earth's crust.

However, some mountains are also formed through effects of erosion. Erosion occurs when wind, rain and ice wear down the surface of Earth.

Different types of mountain are formed in different ways. These mountains also differ in their appearance. Let us take a look at how these different types of mountains are formed.

Fold Mountains

The outermost layer of the Earth, or the crust, is divided into vast plates that fit into each other. These plates are huge pieces of land mass which float over molten rocks present inside the Earth. The plates keep moving a few centimetres every year. There are basically three types of plate movements: one, where plates move into one another; second, where plates move apart; and third, where plates move sideways in relation to each other.

Astonishing fact

The Himalayan Mountain range is the youngest mountain range in the world. It is only 70 million years old, whereas the oldest mountains on Earth, the Barberton Greenstone Belt in eastern Africa, are 3.5 billion years old!

The Himalayan Mountain Range

When two plates move towards or collide with each other, vast areas of the surface of the Earth are uplifted forming folds on top of each other. This process results in the formation of mountains along the boundaries of the two plates. These mountains are known as **Fold mountains**. Fold mountains are vast mountain ranges which stretch for thousands of kilometres. Fold mountains are the most common type of mountains.

Examples of fold mountains include:

- The **Himalayan Mountains** in Asia: The Himalayan Mountains were formed when India crashed into Asia and pushed up the tallest mountain range
- the **Andes** in South America: In South America, the Andes Mountains were formed by the collision of the South American continental plate and the oceanic Pacific plate
- The **Rockies** in North America
- The **Urals** in Russia
- The **Alps** in Europe

The year 2002 was declared the International Year of Mountains by the UN. Since then, December 11 is celebrated every year as the International Mountain Day.

The Alps

Fault-block Mountains

In order to understand a fault-block mountain, it is important to understand what a **fault** is. Faults are simply cracks in the surface of the Earth. The surface of the Earth can move along these faults, and displace layers of rock on either side.

Fault-block mountains (or simply block mountains) are created when the cracks in the Earth's crust break-up large areas of land, pushing materials or blocks of rocks vertically. Due to this, a large mass of land is uplifted and tilted sideways. So instead of folding, as in the case of fold mountains, large pieces of Earth's crusts (or plates) break up and move up or down forming fault-block mountains.

Fault-block mountains usually have a steep front side and then a sloping back side. The uplifted blocks in a fault-block mountain are called **horsts** and the intervening dropped blocks are called **graben**.

There are two types of block mountains – the lifted fault block mountains and the tilted fault block mountains. In a **lifted fault-block** mountain, the mountain has two steep sides. **Tilted fault-block** mountains have a steep side and a gentle sloping side.

Examples of fault-block mountains include:

- the **Sierra Nevada Mountains** in North America
- the Harz Mountains in Germany

The Sierra Nevada Mountains

Dome Mountains

Dome mountains are created when a large amount of magma (molten rock found beneath the surface of the Earth) pushes overlaying rock layers upwards from below the Earth's crust without actually erupting onto the surface. Later on, either the magma cools down or it goes away leaving the pushed up rock as it is. The rock hardens into a dome shape. As the dome is higher than its surroundings, erosion by wind and rain occurs from the top. This results in a circular mountain range.

The **Black Hills** of South Dakota, USA are an example of such a type of mountain formation.

Dome Mountains are also called 'Upwarped Mountains'.

Volcanic Mountains

Volcanic mountains are created by volcanoes. They are formed when molten rock (magma) pushes its way from beneath the Earth to the surface of the Earth and when it reaches the surface it erupts as lava (magma is called lava once it has reached the surface of the Earth), ash, rocks and volcanic gases. These materials get accumulated around the vent through which they erupt. When the lava cools, it builds a cone of rock leading to mountain formation. These mountains are then further shaped by lava flows and other materials thrown out by the volcano.

The Black Hills

Examples of volcanic mountains are:

- **Mount St. Helens** in North America
- **Mount Pinatubo** in the Philippines
- **Mouna Kea** and **Mouna Loa** in Hawaii

Plateau Mountains

Plateaus are large areas of high flat land pushed over 600 m above sea level due to Earth's internal activity or formed by layers of lava. However, the mountains formed out of plateaus are not a result of Earth's internal activity. Instead, they are formed by the erosion caused by running water. The rivers following in these regions cut deep into the ground leaving behind tall mountains. These mountains are usually found near fold mountains. The mountains in New Zealand and the Catskill mountains of New York are examples of Plateau mountains.

Theodolite is the instrument used to measure the height of mountains. These days satellite imagery and Global Positioning System are also used to measure their height.

Catskill Mountains

Mountain climate

The climate on a mountain varies depending on what altitude (how high) you are up a mountain. On mountains the temperature drops rapidly as one starts to move higher. This happens because as the altitude increases, the air on mountains becomes thinner and starts to retain lesser heat as compared to surrounding low lying areas. In more scientific terms, the air pressure on mountains decreases with altitude. As a result of the reduced air pressure, rising air expands and cools.

Astonishing fact

It is estimated that in 10 million years time, the Himalayas will have moved approximately 1,500 km into Asia!

Mountains usually receive more rainfall than the surrounding flat lands. This is because a lower temperature results in lesser evaporation. (Evaporation is the conversion of water from its liquid state to its gaseous state which is known as vapours.) Lesser evaporation means more moisture in the air. As the air full of moisture is carried upward by the winds, it cools even more, and since cool air carries less moisture than warm air, the collected moisture falls in the form of rain.

Mountain weather is prone to dramatic changes in a short period. For example, even when the sky is perfectly clear a thunder storm can occur in a matter of few minutes, and the temperatures can drop from extremely hot to extremely cold in a few hours.

Mountains also drastically affect the climate of the surrounding low lying area. Mountains can block rainfall for areas lying behind them, so that one side of a mountain range may be rainy and the other side may be a desert. Much of airborne moisture falls as rain on the windward side of mountains. The leeward side gets far less rain and remains dry. This effect is called a **rain shadow**. The **windward** side of a mountain is the one which faces the wind carrying air full of moisture. This is the side which receives more rainfall. The **leeward** side is the wind protected side of a mountain. This area receives lesser rainfall.

The higher the mountain more marked the rain shadow effect is. Many deserts of the world were formed because of the lack of moisture blocked by the mountains. The Gobi Desert located behind the Himalaya mountain range in Asia is an example of a desert created due to rain shadow effect.

Due to the sudden changes in temperature and air pressure along a mountain slope, a mountain usually includes two or more regions of climate and plant life at different levels.

The foothills of a mountain may be covered with forests containing broadleaved trees such as poplar, beech, etc. As we go higher up, trees like spruce and pines start to appear. The trees eventually thin out and disappear with the increasing altitude. The highest parts of the mountain support only short grasses and low-growth of Alpine flowers. At an even higher level even this vegetation disappears and the peak is bare and rocky and perhaps covered in snow and ice.

In most parts of the world, a mountain must reach 2,000 feet (600 m) above its surroundings in order to include two or more climate zones. Climate zones found on mountains can be broadly divided into three categories on the basis of the plant life: **Alpine, subalpine** and **montane**. Let us take a look at each of them in detail.

The Gobi Desert

Plant life on mountains can vary from dense jungles which remain green all the year round, to glacial ice within a range of few kilometres.

Alpine

The Cascade Mountains

Alpine climate is the climate found above the tree line on a mountain. Alpine climate is also referred to as mountain climate or highland climate. Alpine climate exists in mountainous regions worldwide.

Tree line is a gradual change in most places. As the level of elevation increases, trees grow shorter due to harsh climate conditions till the time they simply stop growing all together.

The Rocky mountains, the Andes, the Himalayas, the Cascade Mountains, the Tibetan Plateau, and the central parts of Borneo and New Guinea are examples of alpine climate.

The plants found in this region are characterized by short shrubs and grass growing close to the ground. These plants are slow growers. The short summers are used by these plants to store food in their roots in order to survive the chilling cold of winter. Alpine plants flower during the spring season spreading on the surface of the mountain like a carpet of beautiful colours.

Tree line is the edge of the region on a mountain beyond which trees are incapable of growing because of the unsuitable environmental conditions (usually cold temperatures, insufficient air pressure, or lack of moisture).

Tree lines on different mountains vary according to climate, not altitude.

Subalpine

The alpine zone gradually shifts into subalpine zone which is located immediately below the tree-line. Tuolumne Meadows in the Sierra Nevada of California, USA, is a good example of a subalpine meadow.

Trees that grow in this area vary according the location of the zone. Snow Gum in Australia, or Subalpine Larch, Mountain Hemlock and Subalpine Fir found in western North America are all examples of subalpine trees growing in the subalpine zone.

Trees in the subalpine zone often become **krummholz**. Krummholz are a special feature of subarctic and subalpine zones. Continual exposure to fierce, freezing winds causes the stunted and twisted form of these trees. At tree-line, trees may grow on the lee side of mountain and grow only as high as the mountain provides shelter from the wind. Growth thus becomes more horizontal than vertical. Fully grown krummholz trees may be several hundred to thousand years old.

Trees showing Krumholz formation include Balsam Fir, Black Spruce, Subalpine Fir, Subalpine Larch, Engelmann Spruce, Limber Pine, and Lodgepole Pine.

Krummholz trees

The Ethiopian Highlands

Montane

Montane regions are highland regions found below the subalpine zone often isolated from other mountainous regions by warmer, lower elevation regions. The climate is cool, wet and sunny and is home to many distinctive and widespread plants. Rainfall is abundant in these areas. Plants in these regions display features such as waxy surfaces, hairy leaves, etc. The term 'montane' means 'of the mountains'. Montane ecosystems are covered by trees as they lie in regions which have growth suitable temperatures.

The highest known mountain in our solar system is Olympus Mons, a 27,000 m high volcano on Mars.

However, in drier climate conditions, one finds montane grasslands, savannas, and woodland, like the Ethiopian Highlands, and montane steppes like the steppes of the Tibetan Plateau.

What is an ecotone?

An ecotone is the area of boundary between two different plant communities lying alongside such as a forest and a grassland. An ecotone may be narrow or wide. Ecotones are also found in mountainous regions since mountain slopes experience a wide variety of climatic conditions. Mont Ventoux in France is such an example of an ecotone. It marks the boundary between the animal and plant life of northern and southern France.

Uses of mountains

Mountains are rich source of water for our planet. Besides that mountains are also home to innumerable amount of plants and animals which are only found on mountains. Other major uses of mountains are:

- **Tourism:** Tourists from all over the world visit mountains to enjoy the beautiful scenery, the pleasant weather and the exotic animal and plant life. More than 50 million people visit mountains each year.
- **Agriculture:** Mountains also provide land for farming and huge grasslands for the animals to graze on.
- **Electricity:** Mountains naturally provide the elevation required to store water and produce electricity.
- **Wood:** Mountain forests are a good source of wood.

Mountain tourism

Astonishing fact

It has been estimated that 12 per cent of the world's total population live in mountain areas!

Mountains for recreation

Mountains are favourite spots for leisure activities. People visit mountains for relaxation, clean air, beautiful scenery, etc. People are also greatly interested in local traditions and simple life styles of the people living on mountains. Mountains provide a great opportunity for sports that require steep slopes or winter snow such as:

- Skiing

Skiing on snow

- Snowboarding
- Sledging /tobogganing
- Icefall climbing
- Snow-shoe trekking
- Winter walking
- Ice skating

Other than these activities, mountains are also famous for mountaineering, paragliding, hiking, bird watching, rafting, mountain biking etc.

Astonishing fact

The Alps are the most densely populated mountain area in the world. Approximately thirteen million people live in the Alps.

Environmental dangers

Although the popularity of mountains among people has its advantages it can have serious impact on the environment, on the people who live there and the local economy. As more and more people visit the mountains, whether to climb or for other fun activities they pose a serious threat to the environment. People who visit the mountains leave behind tons of plastic waste and other waste materials. As a result various glaciers have started to melt and shrink in size. This is a serious situation as it can lead to melting of major fresh water resources on our planet.

Snowboarding

Snowboarding

Astonishing fact

The people living on mountains have larger hearts and lungs to breathe the thin air at high altitudes.

Major mountain peaks

Asia

Mount Everest (or Sagarmatha)

Height: 8,848 m

Location: Nepal-Tibet border

Mountain range: The Himalayas

First ascent: Sir Edmund Hillary and Tenzing Norgay on May 29, 1953.

Mount Everest is the world's highest mountain above sea level. It was given its official English name in 1865 by the Royal Geographical Society. It was named after the former British Surveyor General of India **Sir George Everest**. The Tibetan name for Mount Everest is 'Chomolungma' which means 'mother goddess of the universe'. The Nepalese government gave Mount Everest the official name 'Sagarmāthā' which means 'goddess of the sky'. Mount Everest was formed along with the Himalayan mountain range as a result of the collision of Indian plate with Asia about 60 million years ago. Mt. Everest still rises a few millimetres each year due to geological forces.

Mount Godwin Austen/K2

Height: 8,611 m

Location: China-Pakistan border

Mountain range: Karakoram Range

First ascent: Italian expedition with Ardito Desio, Lino Lacedelli and Achille Compagnoni, Walter Bonatti and Pakistani Hunza porter Mahdi on July 31, 1954

K2 is the second-highest mountain on Earth after Mount Everest. K2 is also known as the 'savage mountain' because of the difficulties it poses to its climbers. It has the second highest fatality rate among the peaks with a height of 8,000 m or more. Out of every four people who have reached the summit, one has died trying. K2 has never been climbed in winter.

The mountain was named Mount Godwin-Austen in the honour of Henry Godwin-Austen, a previous explorer of the region. Though the name was rejected by the Royal Geographical Society, it is still in use.

Kanchenjunga

Height: 8,586 m above sea level

Location: India-Nepal border

Mountain range: Kanchenjunga Mountain Range

First ascent: Joe Brown and George Band, 'a British expedition' on May 25, 1955

Kanchenjunga is the third highest mountain in the world. The name Kanchenjunga means 'The Five Treasures of Snows', as it contains five peaks. The peaks symbolically represent the five treasures of God, which are gold, silver, gems, grain, and holy books. Kanchenjunga or 'Sewalungma' is considered sacred in the Nepalese religion.

The British expedition which first climbed the peak honoured the beliefs of the local people, by stopping a few feet short of the actual peak. All the successful climbing parties have followed this tradition since then. Kanchenjunga is known for its famous scenic views from the hill station of Darjeeling.

Europe

Mount Elbrus

Height: 5,642 m above sea level (west summit)

Location: Russia

Mountain range: Caucasus Mountain Range

First ascent: A. W. Moore, F. Gardiner, F. Cruford Grove, Horace Walker, Pete Knubel, in 1874

Mount Elbrus is an inactive volcano in the western Caucasus Mountain Range in Russia. Elbrus has a large amount of magma underneath it. However, it is presently considered inactive as no eruptions have ever been recorded. In the Greco-Roman mythology, Zeus had chained Prometheus, the Titan who stole fire from the gods, to these mountains.

Mount Elbrus

Mont Blanc

Height: 4,807 m above sea level

Location: Italy/France

Mountain range: The Alps

First ascent: Jacques Balmat and Michel-Gabriel Paccard on August 8, 1786

Mont Blanc (French) or Monte Bianco (Italian) is the highest mountain in the Alps, Western Europe and the European Union. Its name means, 'white mountain'. It is also sometimes known as 'La Dame Blanche' (French) which means the 'white lady'. The climb of the mountain, marks the beginning of modern mountaineering. The first woman to reach the summit was Marie Paradis in 1808.

The Mont Blanc Mountain and the surrounding peaks are being considered as a possible World Heritage Site because of their importance as the birthplace and symbol of modern mountaineering.

North America

Mount McKinley

Height: 6,194 m above sea level

Location: Alaska, U.S.A

Mountain range: Alaska Mountain Range

First ascent: Walter Harper, Hudson Stuck, Harry Karstens, R. Tatum, in 1913

Mount McKinley is the highest mountain peak in North America and the United States. Mount McKinley was uplifted by the movement of tectonic plates inside the Earth's surface formed. The erosion caused by winds stripped away the softer sedimentary rock above and around the mountain.

Mont Blanc

South America

Aconcagua

Height: 6,962 m above sea level

Location: Argentina

Mountain range: The Andes Mountain Range

Aconcagua is the highest mountain in North and South America and the highest mountain outside Asia. It is located in the Andes mountain range in the Argentine province of Mendoza.

First ascent: Matthias Zurbriggen, in 1897

Aconcagua

Ojos Del Salado

Height: 6,891 m above sea level

Location: Chile

Mountain range: The Andes Mountain Range

First ascent: Alfred Szczepanski and Justyn Wojsznis, Polish expedition, in 1937

Ojos Del Salado

Nevado Ojos del Salado is a huge volcano mountain in the Andes on the Argentina-Chile border. It is the highest volcano in the world. Its name means 'water source of the salty river'. Its name comes from the large deposits of salt that appear in its glaciers in the form of lagoons.

It is also the highest mountain in Chile. The mountain has extremely dry conditions because of the nearby Atacama Desert. Snow remains on the peak only during winter. Despite the generally dry conditions, there is a permanent crater lake about 100 metres in diameter at an elevation of 6,390 m on the eastern side of Ojos Del Salado. This is the highest lake of any kind in the world.

Africa

Kilimanjaro

Height: 5,893 m above sea level

Location: Tanzania

Mountain range: East Africa Mountains, north-east Tanzania

First ascent: Dr Hans Meyer, on October 5, 1889

Kilimanjaro, with its three volcanic cones, Kibo, Mawenzi and Shira, is an inactive volcano and the highest mountain in Africa. It is situated entirely within the borders of Tanzania, close to the border of Kenya. Kilimanjaro is the tallest freestanding mountain rise in the world, rising 4,600 m from its base.

Antarctica

Vinson Massif

Height: 4,892 m above sea level

Location: Antarctica

Mountain range: Sentinel Range

First ascent: Nicholas Clinch, in1966

Vinson Massif (**massif** is a compact group of mountains) is the highest mountain of Antarctica, located about 1,200 km from the South Pole. The mountain is about 21 km long and 13 km wide. The highest point is Mount Vinson.

Vinson Massif

Kilimanjaro

Puncak Jaya

Oceania

Puncak Jaya

Height: 4,884 m above sea level

Location: Indonesia/ New Guinea Oceania

Mountain range: Sudirman Mountain Range

First ascent: Heinrich Harrer, with Temple, Kippaz and Huizenga, in 1962

Puncak Jaya is the highest mountain of Indonesia. It is sometimes also known as Mount Carstensz or the Carstensz Pyramid. The mountain is the highest of Oceania (Australia) and the 5th highest mountain in southeast Asia. It is also the **highest island peak** in the world.

Astonishing fact

Mount Elbrus was climbed in 1956 by a group of 400 mountaineers.

Ten longest mountain ranges

The Rockies

The ten longest mountain ranges of the world have been listed below along with their location and highest peaks:

The Andes

Total length: 7,200 km

Location: South America

Highest peak: Aconcagua in Argentina (6,962 m above sea level)

The Andes Cordillera is the longest mountain range system in the whole world. It stretches through seven countries: Venezuela, Colombia, Ecuador, Peru, Bolivia, Argentina and Chile. The Andes are mostly folded mountains primarily made of limestone, sandstone, slate, and granite. The Andes are home to numerous volcanoes some of which are active. Frequent earthquakes are also an important feature of this range.

The Rockies

Total length: 4,800 km

Location: North America

Highest peak: Mount Elbert (4,399 m above sea level) in Colorado.

The Rocky Mountains, or simply called the Rockies, are located in Western North America extending from north-west Canada to New Mexico.

Andes

The Himalayas

The Himalayas

Total length: 3,800 km

Location: Asia

Highest peak: Mount Everest in Nepal (8,848 m above sea level)

The Himalayas, translated as 'Land of Snow' is home to the highest peaks of the world. The Himalayas form the border of India and Tibet, extending through Bhutan, Nepal, Pakistan and into Afghanistan. Nine of the world's fourteen 8,000 m peaks are located here.

The Great Dividing Range

Total length: 3,600 km

Location: Australia

Highest peak: Mount Kosciusko (2,230 m above sea level)

The Great Dividing Range is located in Eastern Australia. Few of the peaks in this range are higher than 1500 m, even though this is the fourth longest range in the world and includes the Snowy Mountains and the Blue Mountains.

The Great Dividing Range

The Transatlantic Mountains

The Transantarctic Mountains

Total length: 3,500 km

Location: Antarctica

Highest peak: Mount Kirkpatrick (4,528 m above sea level)

Antarctica is the coldest and highest continent on Earth located around the South Pole. Many massive glaciers form part of the Transantarctic Mountains.

The Brazilian Coastal Range

Total length: 3,000 km

Location: South America

Highest peak: Pico da Bandeira near Rio de Janeiro (2,890 m above sea level)

The Brazilian Highlands are actually comprised of various continuous subranges.

The Brazilian Coastal Range

The Sumatra-Java Range

Total length: 2,900 km

Location: In the Indian Ocean (Indonesia)

Highest peak: Mount Kerinci, Sumatra (3,806 m above sea level)

The Sumatra-Java Range extends through the tropical islands of Sumatra and Java. The range consists of 50 active volcanoes located on Java. The highest peak Mount Kerinci is located in Sumatra.

The Aleutian Range

Total length: 2,600 km

Location: Alaska

Highest peak: Mount Shishaldin on Unimak Island (2,861 m above sea level)

The Aleutian Range forms a peninsula in Alaska as a chain of 150 islands, separating the Pacific Ocean from the Bering Sea. The islands are formed by the tops of volcanic mountains.

Aleutian Range

The Tian Shan Mountain Range

Total length: 2,200 km

Location: Asia

Highest peak: Pik Pobedy in Kyrgyzstan (7,439 m above sea level)

The Tian Shan Range forms the border between Kyrgyzstan and China in Central Asia. The name 'Tian Shan' means celestial mountains. Geographers usually divide the Tian Shan into four regions: Central, Northern, Western, and the Inner Tian Shan.

The New Guinea Mountain Range

Total length: 2,000 km

Location: New Guinea Island

Highest peak: Puncak Jaya in Indonesia (5,030 m above sea level)

The New Guinea Mountain range is the tenth longest mountain range. It is located in the Pacific Ocean on the Island of New Guinea. The range moves through the central region of the island and the western part belongs to Indonesia and the eastern part to another country, Papua New Guinea.

Tian Shan Mountain Range

Major mountain ranges

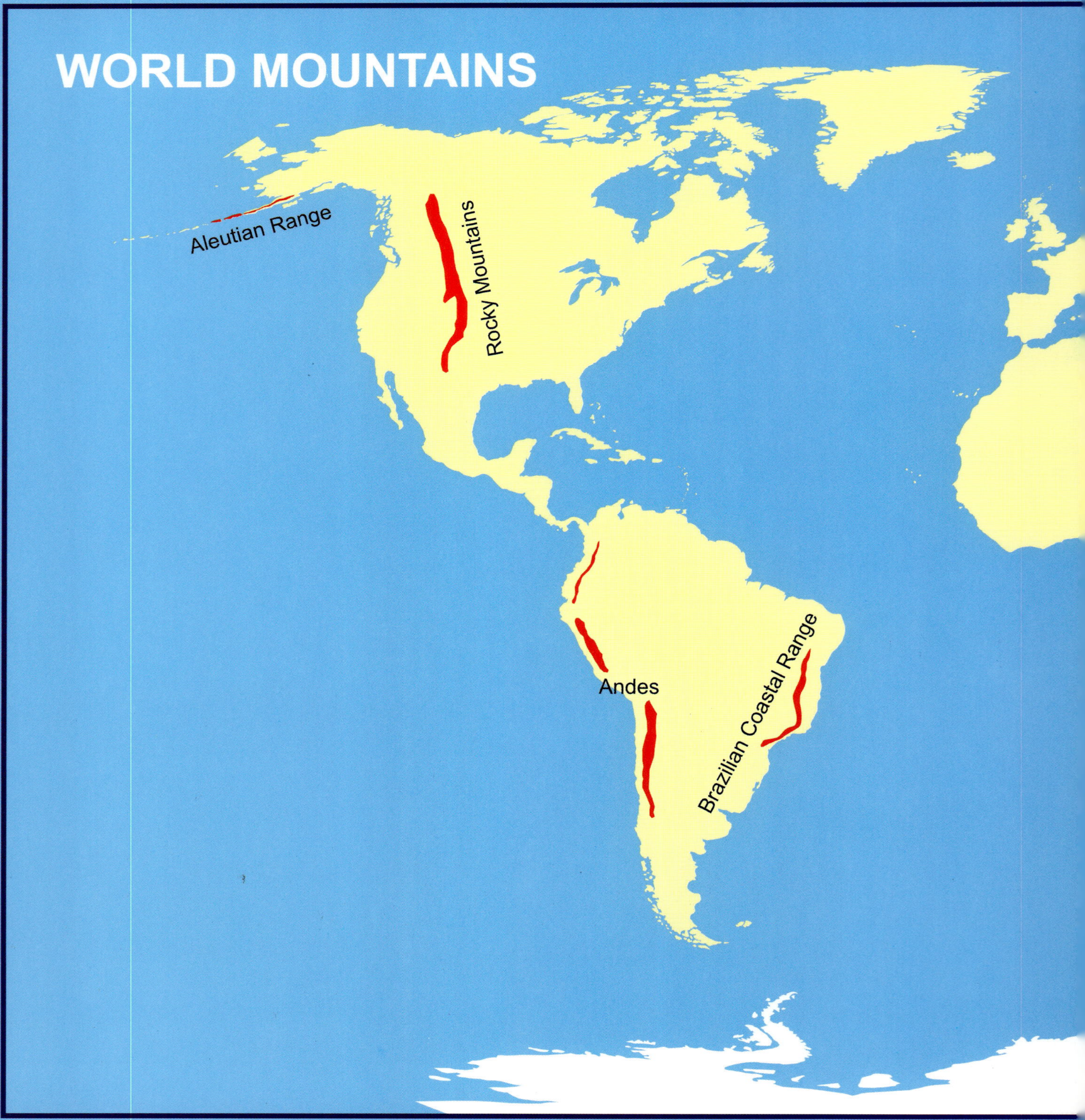

WORLD MOUNTAINS

Aleutian Range

Rocky Mountains

Andes

Brazilian Coastal Range

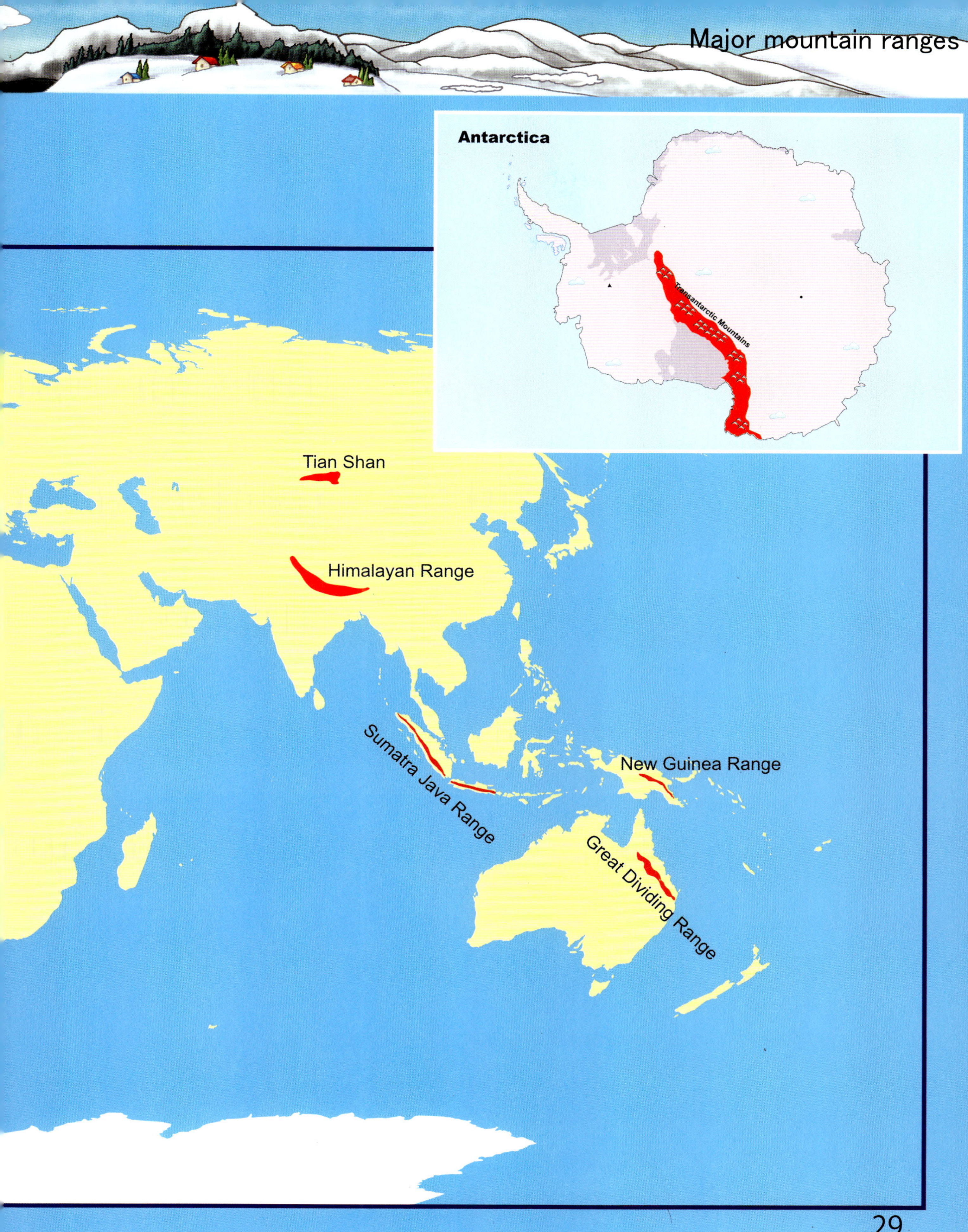
Antarctica
Transantarctic Mountains
Tian Shan
Himalayan Range
Sumatra Java Range
New Guinea Range
Great Dividing Range

Save mountains, save Earth

Mountains are a primary source of water on Earth. Also mountains help in maintaining the ecological balance in nature. However, increasing pollution levels and other factors such as deforestation and global climate change are putting this balance under threat. It is now upon us to take steps to stop the damage being done to our mountains.

As a result of our carelessness, the glaciers of the world are melting on a faster rate than before. The snow on the glaciers normally reflects back most of the sunlight it receives. Presence of more dust, non-biodegradable substances such as plastic, iron etc., cause the ice on the surface of the glaciers to absorb more sunlight and heat since they don't reflect it back.

The rapid melting of glaciers can result in floods at large level and an increase in the sea level. Eventually the Earth may get submerged in water again. Also, rapid melting of the glaciers means more water from our rivers will flow into the sea. This can cause severe water crisis in the times to come.

All of us can do little things which can mean a lot to our environment and our mountains. Whenever you go to the mountains do not throw plastic or any other sort of waste. Bring it back with you. Plastics can take million of years to completely degrade causing pollution on mountains. Since the first successful expedition on Mount Everest, at least 50 tons of trash has accumulated on the mountain.

As the inhabitants of this world, it is not only an ethical responsibility but also a necessity to save the mountains. A threat to our mountains is a direct threat to our existence. Thus, it is crucial that we start acting now to save Earth and ourselves from destruction.

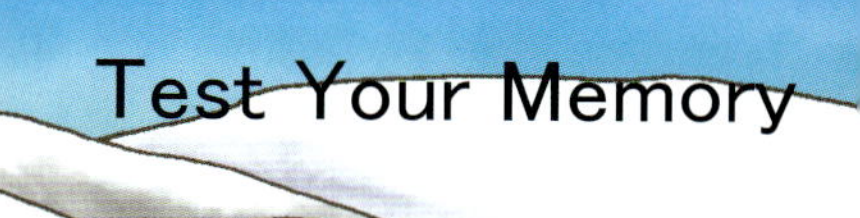

Test Your MEMORY

1. What is the name of the highest mountain on Earth (above sea level)?
2. Name the five basic types of mountains.
3. What is the study of mountains called?
4. Which is the youngest mountain range in the world?
5. When is the International Mountain Day celebrated?
6. Sierra Nevada Mountains in North America are example of which type of mountains?
7. Give an example of volcanic mountains.
8. Name the instrument used to measure the height of mountains.
9. What is the name of the rain shadow area situated behind the Himalayas?
10. Name the three climate zones found on mountains.
11. What is the name of the highest mountain in our solar system?
12. What is the most populated mountain range of the world?

Index

---

* Maps not to scale; for illustration purpose only.